Story n

I am loving this even more than I anticipated- which, is *a lot*! Sparking me in new ways that I could have never even dreamed of before I started, and it has me thinking A LOT about how I started writing.

When I was a kid- I would write until I couldn't possibly write anymore. Young Writers Day was my absolute favorite day of the year. I am going to pretend that you know what I am talking about because I don't want to think about anyone growing up without the joy of Young Writers Day.

Just because I love it so much- I'll tell you what I remember about it and why it was my favorite day.

We got to use our entire class time to work on writing and illustrating our books. Once we were happy with them, it was off to the lamination station where we got to laminate and bind our books.

It felt so permanent.

These pages were sealed forever!

Bound together! I remember thinking, "I made that."

I was so proud.

Then my favorite day of the year would arrive! The day we got to show these babies off!

School wasn't normal that day.

We would have a half day.

The morning was filled with "learning" which was really just talking about how excited we were for the afternoon. Our teacher would slip in a few learning moments here and there, but not really. We dressed up a little and were even allowed to invite people from our families!

When everyone arrived and settled down, we got to share our stories.

They were short stories so everyone that wanted to read out loud – got to.

And afterwards?

We got to show them off to *everybody*.

I was *bursting* with excitement!

It was the best day of the entire year.

I loved every single thing about it.

I knew the minute that I was able to participate in Young Writers Day, that I was in fact, made to write books.

I have known it in my soul for as long as I can remember.

It is honestly the longest that I have ever spent with an idea that I didn't execute or pass by.

It just stays with me.

I can't shake it.

So, I got curious.

I know in my *soul* that writing is for me… right?

So… why haven't I been publishing my writing?

I mean- don't get me wrong.

I have been writing plenty.

But nobody saw anything. Nothing was being published.

I deleted it. I burnt it. I threw it in the trash.

Why?

I really felt a BIG pull here. I asked myself- why the hell am I not an author?

I sat with that feeling for a long time.

I REALLY wanted to pay attention here and the longer I sat- the more I noticed that my body started to hurt in a big way.

I have dealt with chronic pain for the majority of my life.

This was the first time that I started viewing it as a tool and a way to help me instead of this devastating thing that was holding me back.

Don't worry- I've got one of these about pain for you too. But for now- I wanted to know- why the hell was I not an author?

Why hadn't I been trying?

Why did I never reach my dream?

Or really ever even try?

I started thinking about my favorite day of the year and then I realized, it didn't stay my favorite day.

Why did I stop loving it after 4th grade?

If you read my very first published book, The Accident: How to Shake the Sh!t Out of Your Life- then you know,

I'm all about finding the lessons in everything.

This story was the beginning of me finding forgiveness towards myself.

I shed so many tears through writing this, reading this.

I let go of so many big emotions.

The more I healed- the lighter I felt.

And the lighter I felt- the more I realized...

I am not the only one that went through something like this.

This story can shake things up.

This story is powerful.

This story is mine to tell for a reason.

This story.

If this story hits you in the feels – sparks something for you- takes you back to a time in your life – where these big feelings happened to you-

Hear them.

Feel them.

Know that you are not alone.

You are not to blame.

Once we start to acknowledge our stories, we can learn to accept them. We can heal them. We can grow from them.

Your story is yours- and yours alone.

It is powerful.

It is impactful.

It is needed.

I hope this story sparks something - connects you to a time in your life that needs a little love - and helps you through it.

Life isn't always fair- but that doesn't mean it can't still always be beautiful.

Young Writers Day:

4th grade was when life really started to change for me. I had my first run in with a *really* awful teacher. She had been there forever, and she was part of the teacher's union.

I didn't know what that meant then-, but I heard it thrown around a lot as a kid.

She seemed to be untouchable.

One day - I watched her scream in the face of one of my classmates.

I couldn't believe what I was seeing.

My brain couldn't even quite comprehend it.

He was sitting in his chair, and she had leaned in- gripping the back of his chair- screaming at him for disrupting class. I saw her slam a kid up against the wall. I saw her push kids. I heard her say mean, hateful things to other teachers and to the students.

If this was a Disney movie- she would definitely be the villain.

Before I met her- I was lucky.

Really lucky.

School was my favorite place before I met her.

Meeting her was the first time I ever remember feeling afraid of an adult.

I never imagined it would be a teacher.

Teachers and police officers were the good guys!

We were taught that at home, at school, in the movies, on TV.

They were safe.

We could go to them if we were lost, scared, struggling.

Anything.

Until one day, she came along and everything that I had ever learned felt like a lie.

One day- the kids in my class were talking about how scary she was. We had all noticed the shift.

We were getting more nervous each day about going to her class.

We were getting more bad days than good ones.

We all knew we needed to do something, but we didn't know what.

In her class - when we finished our work, we had the option to go over to the reading corner and get a book as long as we weren't disrupting the kids that were still working.

I loved it!

It allowed me to get up and move around a little – and then get lost in a book.

I always hoped that I was done early so that I could read.

And this time- I was lucky and was one of the first ones done!

I usually wasn't one of the first ones done because I'd spend time double checking my work- but this time?

This time I felt really confident about it.

I stood up from my seat and walked to her desk.

I handed her my assignment.

I was so proud- so excited!

She didn't reach for it.

She didn't look up.

Instead, with a disgusted tone she said,

"There is no way *you* have finished this. Did you guess?"

Obviously- she didn't realize it was me standing here. I mean- she hadn't looked up. Once she saw it was me- it would make sense.

So, I did that thing you do- where you kind of duck down and move your body around – trying to get into her line of sight.

But- she still didn't look- or take my paper.

Awkward…

Now I honestly didn't know what to do.

So, me being me- I thought to myself- I know!

I'll make a joke!

I know, right?

A joke.

With Cruella Di Vil.

I responded to her question by starting with a HA! Followed by a sarcastic: "Yeah! *I* just *guessed*." But, I said it like- "Duh! You know I didn't guess. Obviously, I didn't guess. I never guess. I am always prepared. Quit pulling my leg over here and take my paper so that I can go read! "

Here's where we get it all back on track.

She looked up- she realized it was me.

We laughed.

She apologized.

She apologized to the class and told us a story about this *really tough* thing she was going through in her life.

We all understood.

Some slow instrumental music came on.

We all hugged.

She was never mean again.

The end.

That is what I hoped would happen next. I watched A LOT of Full House, Boy Meets World, Growing Pains- Saved by the Bell. If it had a very obvious lesson and some sappy tunes- count me in!

I loved everything about it.

And I KNEW that was the way that life was really supposed to be.

That is the way that my life should always be.

I felt that in my soul.

That feel good everything.

Even the bad moments weren't bad.

They learned- they were honest- they moved forward.

That was what real life was.

It was all I wanted.

More of that feeling.

That was not what I was about to get.

She did not take it as a joke. She slowly looked up and locked eyes with me. She told me- in a very low – very authoritative tone,

"Take it back to your seat, *now*."

I stood there- quiet- confused.

I was nervous.

Everything felt wrong.

I genuinely didn't know what to do. I was really done... Why couldn't I hand it in?

I just wanted to read!

The minute my brain realized that this was taking away from my reading time- I was angry- and my mouth opened before I could even process what I should do.

"Wait, what? I'm just joking. I didn't guess. I'm really done."

She just sat there- not moving.

Eyes locked on mine.

It was weird.

I didn't know what to do. So, I did what I wanted to do.

I wanted to read.

I set the paper down on her desk without breaking eye contact and I turned to walk away to get a book.

She stood up and grabbed my wrist.

It happened so fast- I didn't even see it coming. She caught me completely off guard.

And then-

she *squeezed*.

It shocked me more than it hurt at first. I sucked in my breath and held it as I stared at her hand wrapped around my wrist.

What was even happening?

I just wanted to read.

She told me to pick up my paper- and take it back to my desk.

I was still watching her hand- wrapped around my wrist.

That's all I could focus on. My brain couldn't make sense of why it was there. It shouldn't be there. This was wrong. She jerked my arm down towards her– causing me to lose my stance and step forward. That shook me out of my fixation on her hand and back into the situation.

I watched her lips move as she said:

"There is no way that *you* could **possibly** be done with *this* test."

This moment right here changed everything for me.

Before this moment I loved school.

I loved studying.

I sat at the desk in my room that had been passed down through generations of my family- every single night. I loved that desk. I loved the story of that desk. I loved working on homework, my stories and diving into learning more about the things I had spent my day hearing about.

I took it all in.

I was constantly wanting to play school with my friends or asking people to quiz me on spelling words. I would even jump rope / skip it / play on the monkey bars and incorporate spelling games or try to see how long I could go making history facts or math problems into raps.

I loved to see how far I could get.

Up until this very moment- I never knew that anyone (other than my brother) ever viewed me as anything other than incredibly smart.

She had no reason to think that I was stupid- unless... maybe I wasn't doing as well as I thought?

Maybe she just didn't tell me I was behind?

Maybe I was really far behind and didn't know it?

Was everything a lie?!

Nothing made any sense, and I was frantically trying to make it make sense.

The skin around my wrist started burning.

It drew my attention back to her hand- still holding my wrist.

Why was she grabbing me *so* hard?

It really hurt.

I had to get out of here.

I tried to pull away, but she wouldn't let go.

I started with "but..."

She slammed her free hand down on the desk and squeezed my wrist harder. My wrist was *throbbing*. I couldn't hold my breath through it anymore.

I quickly let it out and yelled out-

"OW!

Let go!"

I tried to rip my wrist away, but she didn't budge.

Instead, she moved in closer to my face -pulling me in towards her with my wrist.

Very quietly – yet crystal clearly- she told me to "take my fucking paper back to my desk- NOW."

I was stunned.

I couldn't move.

I sucked in my breath again and held it.

Some of the other kids noticed it was happening.

You could feel the tension in the room full of kids trying to watch- wanting to help- wanting to pretend it wasn't happening- not knowing what to do.

I could hear them shuffling around in their seats. I knew without looking that most of them were pretending to be hyper focused so they could maybe prevent whatever was happening from happening like I had done so many times before.

I stood there- staring her in the face- air sucked in- mouth closed.

She let go of my wrist. As badly as I wanted to shake it off- pull it away- wrap my own hand around it to keep it safe-

I didn't.

Without breaking eye contact- I slowly reached for- and picked up - my paper. I turned and walked back to my seat. I slouched down in my chair and slowly let the breath out.

I folded my arms on the desktop and put my head down facing the board- away from her. I didn't know what else to do.

I couldn't read now and there was no WAY I was going to fake working on the test.

I made sure that there wasn't a single second that she thought I was working on it.

She was going to know when she graded it that I *aced* it.

She was going to know she was wrong.

I was angry.

I was really upset.

It was one of the first times I remember feeling anxious.

I didn't know what it was then - but I used to always describe it as wanting to jump out of my skin in a bad way. I wanted to jump out of my body, and I couldn't. I wanted to scream, but I couldn't. I would start to feel like ants were dancing under my skin- up my arms- up my shoulders- down my spine- anywhere.

Nothing was safe.

And then it would itch- and start to burn, like they had poison on their feet.

I was spacing off- thinking about how bad I just wanted to go home when I heard a knock on my desk. I looked up and saw my friend. He had his assignment in his hand. He was on his way to hand it in- but passed by my desk to make a face and say "Yikes!"

He wanted me to know it was okay.

He knew she was wrong.

He saw what happened.

He was trying to be there for me and any other time- I would have hugged him and appreciated him so much.

This time though, I was scared.

I shook my head no- but it was too late.

She was already up and had him pinned against the wall in the reading corner.

She started quietly talking to him- and it was weird. Her face was too close to his face, like she had just done to me.

I couldn't stop watching.

I needed to make sure he was okay.

I didn't understand this.

The yelling I understood- she was angry, I know people yell sometimes when they are angry. But the low tone in her voice – the words she chose- it felt dangerous and not in a fun way.

My tiny body was screaming internally that *this* was not right.

The look on my friend's face- I'll never forget it.

He confirmed what my body knew.

I saw the fear all over his face.

The other kids looked and then looked away, just like they did with me. They were back to shifting around in their seats- but staying focused on the task at hand. They didn't want to direct *any* attention to themselves.

I could tell some of them were done and were just waiting for the bell to ring. Some were erasing answers and rewriting them in.

They weren't even going to try to get a book today.

I remember thinking, - what a stupid day this is turning out to be.

My friend was new, and he was in trouble all the time from the minute he walked in.

He was a good kid though.

It didn't make sense in my brain.

He made me laugh all the time. He was sweet- he was so nice- he was creative.

I loved being around him.

He was one of my very best friends and I let everyone know right away that he was one of us.

He fit right in.

It was like he had been there forever.

The kids were on board.

The teachers though?

The teachers were so quick to label him as a bad kid.

They didn't want to help him. They just wanted to tear him apart.

I hated it.

How could they not see the same boy that I saw?

Seeing him pinned up against the wall by an adult made me angry like I had never felt before.

I was mad about what she did to me- but this, I had never experienced anything like this.

I wanted to hit her.

Shove her away from him.

Pummel her with my fists until she let him go.

I wanted to get up and scream fire into her face.

I saw her stand straight up and walk back to her desk.

He stood there for a few seconds. With his eyes on the floor- he walked back to his desk.

He laid his head down and was quiet the rest of the time. We all sat quietly and waited for the bell to ring, and we all prayed for time to move fast.

This afternoon would be better.

Recess was soon.

The break would do us all some good.

All would be forgotten.

We just had to hang on a little bit longer.

Recess did the trick.

We all got back to class refreshed and took our seats.

We were quiet- ready and determined to have a better afternoon.

She came in and went straight to her desk. She didn't say a word and it felt weird. She looked calm- but she didn't feel calm.

It was eerie.

Nothing happened though.

We got through our lessons and before we knew it- we were done with her for the day.

It all seemed like it was going to be fine despite the fact that it didn't feel fine.

Then she said my friends name quietly and asked him to stay after class.

I couldn't leave him there – it didn't feel right.

I tried to lag behind.

She waited though.

She waited and then told me to hurry up when I really started dragging my feet.

I pretended not to notice that she was trying to rush me out and I asked her if she needed any help with the classroom.

I was looking for any excuse not to leave.

She said no and to get to class. They needed the room to discuss grades.

He looked at me and nodded. It was okay.

I needed to get out of there.

He would be okay.

I couldn't leave- but... I had to.

So, I left.

What she didn't know was that I stayed right outside the door.

When I walked around the corner to hide- I found out that some of our friends had the same feeling.

They were waiting too.

We looked at each other- knowingly- and stayed quiet.

We listened hard to make sure that he was okay.

But he wasn't okay.

We heard it first- the sound of the chair sliding across the floor and slamming into the wall.

One of our friends immediately jumped up and when he peeked through the window his face turned pale.

I realized he was scared of what he saw.

I had never seen him scared before.

Ever.

He was my wildest, bravest friend.

He whispered to me to look, *now*. I realized he was trying not to scare the other kids. I slowly stood up and walked quietly to door. I got up on my tiptoes to see in.

She was too close to his face like before. She was quiet again. She had him pinned up against the wall and this time he was in the chair. She was leaning over him in the chair and his hands were gripping the armrests.

I couldn't stop staring at his wrists.

Why wasn't he moving his hands?

What was on his wrists?

On the chair?

And then I realized that he had duct tape around his wrists.

My heart was pounding in my chest. It felt like it was about to beat through.

Everything in me wanted to start screaming no.

It makes me so sick even thinking about it now.

His face, I will never forget the fear in his face.

He was crying.

Not sobbing- not out of control.

These were tears he was fighting to stop.

Tears he never wanted to fall.

Slow, awful tears that seeped out and slid down his cheeks.

He was trying to keep his cool.

He was trying not to show his fear, but it was creeping out of his eyes and in his body language.

He was so tense.

It wasn't right.

This was going to get worse- I could feel it.

The next thing I knew I was in the classroom.

I don't remember opening the door.

I don't remember moving my body through the threshold.

All of my friends were gone- but I don't remember them leaving.

All I know is that one minute I was in the hallway watching this happen- and the next I am standing in the room that I spent so much of my 4th grade life in- but it didn't feel the same anymore.

She wasn't just scary anymore.

She looked like a monster to me now.

I was devastated.

And the energy in that room…

The energy.

It was like nothing that I had ever felt. The room was filled with a mix of hate and fear that, up until this very moment- I had never felt in my entire life. At the same time though- I felt prepared. Like I always knew that this moment would come and when it came- it wasn't a feeling that was going to make a quick exit from my life.

I was staring at my friend- dead in the eyes- and I took a deep breath in and out.

I did it again and looked at him hard. I wanted him to *feel* what I was saying and what I was saying was "Breathe with me- pull yourself together because we have got to get out of here. I will not leave. Nothing bad will happen with me here."

I was not going to let anything bad happen to him, no matter what.

He looked at me and the tears started falling faster- I shook my head slightly no- and I breathed in again. This time he did it with me.

Message received.

In the time that it took my brain to catch up and realize that my body had moved into the war zone- she had pulled the tape off his wrists.

It was off the second I came through the door.

I glanced at her quickly and noticed that it was still balled up in her hands.

She had taken it off- balled it up and started walking towards the trashcan the second the door opened.

She realized it was me and not an adult on her way over.

She tossed it in and asked me what I needed.

Like everything was just fine.

Like this was normal.

Just be cool Bree.

I wouldn't look at her.

I kept my eyes locked on my friend and said that I needed him for a project. Our teacher told me to come get him right away. We couldn't start until he came back.

I nodded at him to get up and come with me.

He stood up and she grabbed his wrist so hard and pulled him behind her.

She got right up into my face for the second time that day and said, "go back to class NOW you disrespectful little bitch."

It shocked me to my core.

It shouldn't have- but it did.

I never expected anyone to talk to me like that.

I mustered up more courage than I even knew I had and looked her dead in the eyes. I balled my fists and said-,

"Then I guess I'll have to tell him what is happening in here."

If looks could kill- I'd be dead.

She laughed. Just a little- "heh."

Disbelief- shock?

I think that's what it was.

She let go of his wrist. She turned and walked back to her desk. She sat down and said "Go."

She never looked at us again.

It should have felt like a win.

We stood up to the bully!

The good guys always win!

Instead, it felt like the calm before the storm.

She broke us both. She broke a lot of kids. She put some real - awful - trauma into our lives.

And honestly- life would have been a lot better without it. Without her.

We knew we deserved so much better than her, but this was what we had.

We made the best out of it- and hey, at least we banded together.

After that- she left us alone for the most part.

Every time I would see her after that she would tell me with her eyes that it wasn't over.

She wasn't forgetting and she wasn't impressed.

This wasn't the last of it.

But I was determined to get through this.

I had *always* been a good kid.

I didn't make waves around her because her energy scared me.

Up until that day- I wanted her to like me.

I would do anything she needed.

I would erase the board and clean up the room- pick up the chairs, whatever I could do to help.

I didn't want to be on her radar when she was mean.

It had been successful up until I finished my test early (the nerve!) and barged in on her.

Suddenly all the good things that I had done – were for nothing.

I was officially on her list.

I kept my head down.

I was quiet.

I got in and out of her class each day.

Maybe she would just forget.

Move on.

That worked until Young Writers Day.

We had a substitute teacher. We had her before and she was a fine substitute for study hall or a class where you had to pop a movie in and sit back.

She was more like a babysitter - last call if nobody else was available.

Which was fine.

Normally- we looked forward to a movie day but today we did not want to watch a movie.

We were so excited!

We wanted to talk about who was coming in to see our books- what we wrote about- what it looked like- what color of paper we used and what image we chose for our cover.

You know- the important things!

She was not interested in letting us talk about our books that morning.

I know- because I was the one that asked.

She told us to be quiet and watch the movie or we would have to stay in at recess. We all groaned and sat back.

By the time recess rolled around, we were crazy balls of energy. We were bursting at the seams to get up- run around and talk about our exciting afternoon!

Nobody was lining up quietly.

Nobody was standing in a straight line.

We were jumping around!

Everyone's chatter was getting louder and louder.

And suddenly,

She started tearing up.

I felt the room shift- and I immediately wanted to help her.

I felt bad that nobody was listening, So I made a joke- like I always did, and I said "I thought you were a teacher! You gotta scare these kids into line!" Big smile on my face- laughing- very non-threatening- trying to show her– I am just joking with everything I have.

I wanted to make her laugh instead of cry.

There were even arm motions!

Then I yelled to the class- "HEY! Show her some respect! Get in line so we can get outta here!"

Everyone listened- because honestly, everyone always listened.

My voice is loud- it carries.

It always worked.

It was how I helped in every class.

I'd make it funny- everyone would laugh- and then they would listen- and I would say- alright, here's what we need to do- and we'd all do it.

Teachers loved it- they would tell me how much easier I made things when I did that. Even thanked me!

I thought I would make her whole day.

But then…

She started bawling.

I was shocked!

She left the room and we just stood there – looking around at each other not sure what to do. A few seconds went by, and everyone started talking again. I looked at them and quietly- but sharply said- "guys- just shh."

This was serious.

I felt it.

I was nervous.

The ants were back under my skin. I noticed part of the skin on my wrist was turning red.

The burning feeling started to build and then it started to itch like crazy.

The next moment was terrible.

The next moment of my life took away so much of who I was for so long.

This one moment changed everything.

Our substitute did not come back.

I felt it shift before she even walked in the door.

There she was. The "I put my hands on children" teacher.

Her.

She stormed into the room and yelled at everyone to shut up and get in line.

I knew.

I knew she was there for me.

I knew I wasn't going out to recess.

My entire body felt weighted.

My chest sank.

But,

I didn't feel scared.

I felt a weird rush of surrender wash over me.

It felt like I knew that what was about to happen- already happened. No matter what I did in this moment- I knew she would steal part of me, from me.

My body didn't feel good.

I felt like I had the flu.

My skin hurt.

My bones ached.

I felt an overwhelming rush of sadness.

I didn't even do anything wrong.

She told everyone to go outside and get to recess.

I put my head down and jumped in with a few kids.

I tried to blend in and walk past her.

She grabbed onto my upper arm so hard and pulled me out into the hallway.

She never let go of my arm.

My friends looked at me and I nodded that it was

okay.

I was okay.

Just go.

I didn't want this coming back on them.

I didn't want it to be worse for them.

It was my turn.

I just had to take it.

And I knew there was nowhere for them to hide.

We were in the hallway.

They had to go. There was nothing else to do.

I should have started screaming in the hallway.

I should have thrown my body around if she tried to shut me up.

I should have done anything.

But,

I didn't.

I couldn't.

I was frozen.

It already happened. I knew it – this had to happen.

What I didn't realize was that - while this was always going to happen- I did not have to handle it like I did.

But I didn't know that then.

Hindsight and all that.

Let's also recognize that I was a kid, in a small town.

I didn't exactly have the tools developed yet to deal with this kind of trauma.

I took a big breath in and out. I watched the kids- laughing – joking in line.

I kept breathing in and out watching them walk away until the last shoe stepped onto the outside pavement and the door slowly closed behind them.

Nobody was in the hallway.

I could feel that nobody was coming.

It was the perfect storm and whatever was going to happen-

was going to happen.

She whipped my body around so that I was facing towards her and shoved me hard backwards into the wall.

I wish I could say that I was shocked- but I knew it was coming.

I had seen her do this so many times before to other kids.

It was the first time though that an adult had ever physically put their hands on me.

The wrist grab- as messed up as it was, this felt different.

I knew that was wrong, but I also knew that it was something that could happen in the heat of the moment.

I knew that.

But this?

This was straight up wrong.

I couldn't even defend myself.

I was just a kid.

I sucked in some air and thought- hey,

I've always loved a good David vs. Goliath story.

Maybe this was mine.

My brother hit me a lot when we were kids. He was the one person in my life who ever put hands on me- and he had effectively done it enough that I actually felt a little encouraged in this moment.

Like- hey! I have experience here! I know what to do! I know what makes him more mad- and what makes him cool off faster.

I can get through this okay.

Keep breathing.

Just think of your brother.

It's not a teacher. It's your brother.

I made the mistake of regaining my composure. Standing up straight instead of staying on the wall she had shoved me into.

I had gotten a little bit of pep in my step when I thought of her as my brother because he would hit me and leave. He didn't stay and pound on me. So, when she pushed me- I thought maybe that was it- and I stood up so she could yell at me for whatever it was she was there to yell at me for, and maybe still have a chance to get some recess.

I could get through this.

I didn't even know why she was mad at me.

I helped get everyone lined up. I had no idea why the substitute was crying? Or why she went to get her?

She took me standing back up as me trying to show her that I was challenging her- showing her that I wasn't scared instead of ready to listen.

She shoved me hard back into the wall and then she pinned me to the wall by putting her hands on each side of my head. She moved in closer to me. She bent both arms in at the elbows so she could be right in my face, leaving me feeling suffocated with no room to move or breathe.

That feeling of someone bigger and older than you- boxing you in.

I wouldn't wish that on anyone.

She told me that I was a little bitch, and that I would get what was coming to me.

She couldn't believe that I thought that I could "shoot my fucking mouth off to teachers" and it was "time that I learned my lesson." I was too stupid to understand anything, but she was going to make sure that I learned to keep my mouth shut.

Adults had never sworn at me or talked to me like this. Adults had never gotten into my personal space like this.

Nobody had ever made me feel this kind of gross all the way through.

I tried to close my eyes, but she slapped my cheek - just hard enough to sting -*just* a little bit.

Just threatening enough to show me that she was in control.

She told me to look at her while she was talking.

I wasn't expecting that at all.

And it scared me into a whole different world.

So, I did.

I looked right at her.

But I didn't see her.

It was the first time in my life that I can remember disassociating- having an out of body experience.

I didn't know what I was doing then- but when I described it later- I found out what it was.

I can't remember what else she said. I just let her whisper every awful thing that she had to say about me and kept breathing.

In and out.

In and out.

That was what my body did.

Her words faded out.

I couldn't hear.

I wasn't afraid anymore.

In fact, I wasn't anything.

I couldn't feel anything.

I was so relaxed.

It almost felt like I was floating in water.

For a few seconds, my ears were in the water muffling all the sounds. I couldn't even feel anything on my body.

I slipped out so quietly that I didn't even realize any of this until I wasn't there anymore.

I wasn't in the water.

I was floating in the air.

I was watching my body.

I was watching her.

I couldn't look away.

I couldn't think about what I was seeing.

I watched.

I floated.

Feeling nothing at all.

I took in her body language. The way she would only move her hands off the wall to put them really close to my face like she was going to hit me.

I looked so little.

Breathing in.

Breathing out.

Eyes staring at her- with nothing behind them- just trying to get through this.

Then it all hit me.

I realized I was watching me, and I felt confused.

I started feeling tingly.

Then I was overwhelmed with sadness.

Everything was different now.

This wasn't right.

This wasn't normal.

This should never happen.

And all of a sudden I felt sick.

And then?

And then it felt like I was being shot into space.

The next thing I knew- I was back in my body and she was still going.

She had her fist clenched and was shaking it next to my face.

I was going to throw up.

I dipped underneath her arms, and I ran.

I ran into the bathroom, and I threw up.

Then I threw up again.

I sat there- breathing hard- listening to see if she followed me in.

She didn't.

I guess when she heard me throw up- she called it a win and went back to her day.

I slowly pushed myself up off the ground.

I was shaking.

Breathe in- breathe out.

Breathe in- breathe out.

I stood there- just breathing until I felt strong enough to move.

I walked down to the nurse's office and asked her to call my mom to come get me.

I told her I threw up.

I needed to go home.

That was it.

I didn't say a word about what had just happened in the hallway.

I was a frequent flyer to the nurse's office, but I never went home.

I loved school even more than I loved ice packs and Band-Aids.

It was my favorite place to be, and I never wanted to miss a second of it. If anything- I wanted to stay late!

My mom had me get on the phone because this wasn't normal- and it was Young Writers Day.

I told her I didn't feel good and that I was sick, and I swear to you- she probably doesn't even remember- but that day- she knew I was off.

She asked me again- if anything else was happening and I said no- I'm just sick and need to go home.

I asked her to please come get me.

I was already sad enough, I didn't need to talk about it- which, at the time, was the truth.

I had buried it away.

Just like I did with my brother when he was really mean to me.

I stuffed it down and I moved on.

It was over.

It happened.

I had to just keep moving.

This wasn't the last time I'd see her- and that?

That made me want to be sick permanently.

My mom picked me up and I slept the rest of the day and night.

I missed Young Writers Day.

I didn't share my story.

I threw it in the trash.

After that- I was different.

I didn't love school anymore.

And it didn't get better.

I spent the next few months pretending nothing had ever happened when I saw her. I was quiet. I participated when she asked us to.

Instead of getting a book from the reading corner- I started drawing and writing stories instead.

I would keep my paper until she told us to finish up. I wasn't making that mistake again.

Finally- I made it.

The year was over.

I was so happy to be leaving fourth grade behind.

I might still see her- but, I NEVER had to deal with her for class anymore.

I could avoid her.

I could breathe again.

Or so I thought…

We always had a few choices for who we could get as our teachers for the next year.

Usually, all of them were nice. It didn't really matter who you got. It was more about if your friends were with you.

4th, 5^{th,} and 6th grade were different.

Those years- you knew, some kids were having a good year while the other kids would be absolutely miserable.

Those years- you hoped and prayed that you and your friends got the nice teachers.

But after 4th grade-

I was determined to make best of it-

no matter who I got.

I was *certain* that it wouldn't matter.

I would work hard.

I would participate.

I would study.

I would be fine.

Then I learned why nobody wanted this particular teacher for math in 5th grade.

It wasn't because she didn't know what she was doing.

She was the worst teacher because- if she didn't like you or if you didn't pick up what she was putting down immediately?

That was it.

She wasn't going to teach you.

Of course- this is who I was going to spend my 5th grade math life with.

The worst possible teacher for me to have.

Looking back- I shouldn't have been surprised.

Hindsight and all that, right?

I walked up the first day of class – ready to impress.

She was standing outside her door along with the 6th grade math teacher – who was also known for being a teacher that you did not want to get.

But like I said- I was determined to make it a great year.

I thought to myself- hey! This actually works in my favor!

I could win them both over on the very first day!

Then I wouldn't have to be worried about 6th grade either!

I was confident.

I was bubbly.

I was energized.

I was ready.

I walked up to them and warmly said hello- using their names and nodding to them accordingly.

I introduced myself and said how excited I was for the year. I couldn't wait to see what was in store for us! Turning towards the 6th grade teacher I said, "And hopefully, I have you next year!"

They looked at each other and then back to me.

Never smiling.

My new 5th grade teacher spoke first. All she said was:

"We've heard about *you*."

The 6th grade teacher followed up in a disgusted tone:

"I'd rethink your wishes about next year."

She told my 5th grade teacher good luck- nodding back at me – and walked away- heading back to her class.

My chest sank.

I was so sad.

I felt like I couldn't win.

I wasn't a bad kid.

I didn't even do anything wrong.

This was the worst year yet. Things that I didn't even know were an issue at the time- were starting to show up in a lot of big ways.

I had hit my head over the summer and at the time-
I hadn't linked these two things together.

All I knew was that school was a lot harder this year.

I couldn't connect this new math in my brain. I needed help and I was determined to get it. I was not going to fall behind.

I was never afraid to ask questions until 5th grade math.

She had just finished up a lesson on the board and told us to use the rest of our class time to work on our assignment from our book.

I wasn't understanding any of it.

I was completely lost.

I was so happy she gave us class time to work on it.

I walked up to her desk and asked if she could give me another example.

She pointed to what she had put on the board.

I told her that I didn't understand the lesson and asked if she could please explain it to me another way.

She took an irritated sigh and said-

"You should give up now."

"Give up what?" I replied

"Math. You aren't getting it now- and you never will. Take your seat. The example is on the board."

That was it.

I couldn't believe it.

I wanted to cry.

I had never felt so defeated.

I honestly didn't know until that moment that a teacher could even tell you no when it came to asking for help.

I thought that they *had* to help you if you asked.

It was their job to teach it to you a million different ways until one of them stuck.

It never even occurred to me that a teacher- wouldn't want to teach.

That was how my entire year went.

Me asking questions because I didn't understand

and her telling me that I was stupid.

That she couldn't teach me.

That I was on my own.

Quit math.

Quit trying.

I gave up on myself.

Right then and there.

I quit.

I found out that ants under my skin- were not ants.

I had developed hives and they were out of control.

I'd get them all over my body.

My entire body would swell and burn and itch like crazy.

Everyone started making jokes about how I always had hickies on my neck and I hated that.

I hated that all my friends were starting to "date" each other.

I hated that everyone was growing up.

I just wanted to roller-skate without someone telling me that so- and-so wanted to make out with me in the game room.

I wanted adults to be nice.

I just wanted to be a kid.

I wanted to go back to life before all of this.

So far, all I knew – was that growing up sucked.

My math teacher developed a habit of only calling on me if I didn't know the answer.

If I raised my hand- she would not call on me.

I genuinely tried to answer when I knew the answer.

I thought that if I could get a few right- she would back off -

but that wasn't the case.

When she could see me struggling - she would always call on me.

You could hear it in her tone.

You could see it on her face.

The room would change.

The other kids knew it, too.

They could feel it or had experienced it firsthand.

She would call on me.

I would get it wrong.

She would tell the entire class not to be stupid like me.

I was breaking down.

I was shutting myself away.

My body was screaming at me that we were not okay.

But I didn't know what to do.

I wasn't the only kid experiencing this. We all understood. We were all in this together.

The fact that none of us had been able to make it stop- that sealed it in for me that we didn't have any power.

We had to just get through it. Surely one of us would have gotten someone involved if we thought that it would make these teachers help us- right?

Every time I saw her in the halls, every time I knew she was going to switch to class participation- I felt like I was going to puke.

I was sweating.

I couldn't stop breaking out in hives.

I was a ball of anxiety- but I didn't know that.

I had no idea how to voice it.

I thought it was just normal, part of growing up.

The doctors checked me out and said I was fine.

Allergies. Take Benadryl. You'll be good to go.

Benadryl made me fall asleep.

I fell asleep through entire classes.

Who even cared anymore?

One day, I walked into math with a spearmint cough drop in my mouth.

I was under the weather.

I was always under the weather.

I rolled around with cough drops in my bag all the time. My throat was constantly bothering me - it was hard to swallow sometimes- but the doctor checked me out.

Everything was "fine."

I popped in a cough drop because I'd be damned if I was going to start coughing in her class and draw attention to myself.

I drew attention to myself anyway.

She thought it was gum.

And she lost her marbles.

She started yelling at me in front of the entire class about how disrespectful I was.

Who did I think I was chewing gum in her class?!

She said that everything she had ever heard about me was true. Nobody should ever want to be like me. I was stupid and she didn't even know how I was allowed to be in her class.

I would be nothing.

When she was done- she told me to get up and go spit my gum out.

I put it between my teeth and showed her that it wasn't gum. I popped it back into my mouth and said, "It's a cough drop."

I felt so cool.

I had her.

Who was stupid now?

She paused – our eyes were locked.

I smiled.

I had her.

And then she smirked, and I knew- whatever was coming – wasn't good.

"You are *so* smart. What is the solution to the problem on the board?"

Of course.

She knew I didn't know. She wouldn't teach it to me.

She laughed.

The class awkwardly looked around at each other not really knowing what to do.

I felt like I was dead inside.

I didn't care about anything anymore.

I was depressed.

There was nothing good here.

I spent a lot of time in my favorite teacher's room whenever I could.

She would let me hang out in her room during free time to work on homework, work on my stories or if I wanted to come in and read, I could.

I always felt welcome there.

She let me help before and after school if I was early or staying late.

Her room was a safe space.

I didn't tell her much at first.

Most of the time- she would be grading papers while I was doing my thing.

Sometimes I would share my stories with her, and we'd talk about them but for the most part- it was just about feeling safe.

But that's the thing about safe spaces. They are only safe with nobody else really in them.

We were in class working through a lesson.

My favorite teacher had us each read a portion out loud.

I hated when we had to read out loud. For someone who loves to talk- write- read- that's probably surprising. But I hated it. It felt like enormous amounts of pressure. I didn't want to mess up any words.

She called on my cousin and I instantly felt for him.

As much as I hated it- he had a stutter.

He really hated it.

He made it through his part- and I was really proud of him.

We finished up and lined up for recess.

While we were in line- one of the boys in my class decided that it would be hilarious to start making fun of my cousin by imitating his stutter and then exaggerating it.

That made my blood boil.

These kids were nice kids before.

Why were they all getting meaner by the minute?

I locked eyes with him and told him to stop.

Now.

He started laughing- stuttering harder and saying wh-wh- what ah-ah -are yuh-yuh- you go-go-go

Before he could even finish his sentence- my hands were moving.

I shoved him into the coatrack.

He stood back up and started laughing.

He turned to my cousin and said

Ohhhh – I didn't realize you can't talk, and you need a girl to fight your battles!

My fists were balled up.

They moved so fast I couldn't even think.

I punched him square in the face.

His hands went up immediately.

He was bleeding.

Everyone got quiet.

Our teacher walked back in the room and saw what was happening.

She ran over and quickly checked him out. Realizing that he was okay- but needed to get cleaned up- she sent him down to the nurse.

My teacher- my favorite teacher- told me that I was in trouble and that I had to stay inside.

I was so sad.

There goes my safe space.

But then I remember what a jerk that kid was.

I puffed my chest out.

I would regret nothing.

The minute they left- my teacher looked at me and she said-

What the heck!?

This isn't you.

Tell me what happened!

I fell apart.

What hadn't happened?

Everyone sucked.

Everyone was mean.

I was not meant for this world.

I just wanted it to be nice.

I just wanted to learn.

My brain didn't feel like it was working right.

My body constantly felt like it was working against me.

I was behind.

I was never going to be able to catch back up.

People were making me mean.

And now?

Now my safe space was ruined because some stupid kid thought that making another kid feel like complete trash about something that already makes him struggle and feel different- was a cool thing to do.

And the rest of the class felt like backing up that asshole was right thing to do.

And now I was in trouble.

I had no regrets about punching that guy.

I kind of felt like punching all of them.

Let's see how funny things are then.

Assholes.

I hated people.

Why were they so mean?

I didn't want to do *this* anymore.

Everything was so complicated.

I was so tired.

The harder life got- the smaller I felt.

Tears were streaming down my cheeks.

In a rush- I let it all out.

I caught my favorite teacher off guard that day.

She let me cry until I couldn't anymore.

I *wept* that day.

When I finally calmed down she handled what happened first.

She told me that if I kept reacting with my fists- I was going to end up in a lot of trouble and that life, wasn't for me.

She wasn't even mad at me for what I did.

In fact- she was more disappointed that it happened at all.

She also told me that there were people in every profession that shouldn't be there.

That shouldn't cancel out all the good ones though.

She made me realize that focusing on the bad guys?

That's how they win.

I wasn't going to let them have power over me

anymore.

I could get through this.

I could win.

I'd focus on the good.

Get through the bad.

When I started coming into her room from now on-

we were working.

She was helping me with math as much as she

possibly could.

Even though I was still too far behind- and I wasn't really making enough of the information stick in my brain to succeed, I took in just enough to pass.

They couldn't fail you in elementary- so I moved right along.

6th grade came and went, and it was the same thing but not quite as bad.

What changed?

I started turning my sadness into humor. I started looking for the good.

They can't break me if I can make it funny.

And listen- I was *funny*.

And when I was focusing on the good things- I could make *anything* funny.

Nobody told me what to do and I didn't get in trouble because I didn't ever cross the line.

When I got close- I just made them laugh.

It worked.

The kids didn't think about how stupid I was or my hives when they thought of me anymore.

They thought about how funny I was.

I also found- it made me more likable, so when teachers said mean things to me or about me- the kids didn't laugh anymore.

They were on my side.

They liked me and I made them laugh.

Why would someone be mean to me?

This is also the time that I really started to lean into my love of the breeze in- breeze out lifestyle.

I liked to come into the room- make people laugh, and then leave. Mostly because I worked pretty damn hard to be funny and athletic so that people saw those things about me.

If I stayed too long- one of two things happened.

1-   I disappointed them.

Or

2-   They disappointed me.

I would disappoint them by not being everything that they wanted or thought I was.

They would disappoint me because I was disappointed in the world.

They were mean. Mean to each other. Mean to themselves. Mean to faces and even worse behind backs.

Their idea of funny was setting up heartbreak.

So many times, they would get a girl to come over and make them think that they wanted to hang out. They would start talking and say that someone liked them and ask what they thought.

They would try to convince them about why they should like him back.

Once they said okay- yeah, I guess he is nice- I like him too. They would send her over to say, hey- I like you too and watch as he said- what? I never said that I liked you.

Then they would laugh at her while her heart broke and make her seem stupid like she just went over and did this all on her own.

Out of the blue.

These were kids that had been wonderful before. People that I thought were amazing- fantastic people and now this was what they were choosing to do?

What happened to them?

Everyone sucked. Life was full of disappointments. It was better to just find a few people you like and breeze in and breeze out.

So that's what I did.

I started making life fun again.

I was playing outside with my friends a lot.

During the day we'd play capture the flag, kickball- football- anything.

At night we played my favorite game- Jailbreak.

If you don't know what that is- it's basically an amplified mashup of tag and hide-and-go-seek.

I got better at softball and was practicing or playing any chance I got.

We'd shoot hoops in my driveway - meet up at the park- ride our bikes around town.

Anything that felt good, I was in.

I laughed a lot.

I didn't feel so sad anymore.

I had control of math class now. My 6th grade teacher was the weakest link of the three.

The minute I realized I could make jokes every time that she called on me- the game changed.

The whole class would start getting rowdy.

I was a bad influence.

She stopped giving me power in the only way that she could.

She couldn't call on me anymore.

I could breathe.

I could relax.

I was still going into my favorite teacher's room and working on math- doing everything that I could to try to make it stick with my free time.

The only way that I was even going to skate by was by working at it as often as possible.

I did all the practice work I could get my hands on.

It was working.

I was making enough stick to confidently get by.

That felt good.

If you have ever earned an incredibly hard-earned C, then you *know* how good that feels.

The pressure lifts.

You are average instead of behind.

You can breathe a little easier.

Life was looking up.

It would all be okay.

I had taken my power back from the mean teachers.

The good guys always win.

Until- they don't.

It was a beautiful day.

We went over to my aunt and uncles' house late that afternoon.

My cousins, brother and I would hang out while our parents got some adult time.

Typically- we'd break into two groups and not hang out together.

My cousin that was the same age as me, his little brother and I would hit the park behind their house.

I loved it.

It's one of my most favorite things about my childhood.

The park was next to a church and the two of them were surrounded by houses.

The neighborhood kids would show up whenever they could.

It was so much fun.

It had a double swing that was so dangerous. We were obsessed with that thing.

We loved to see how high we could get before we had to bail out and yell "Let go!"

On this beautiful day, my brother and my older cousin decided to come to the park with us.

Which was weird.

They never wanted to hang out with us at home let alone at the park.

We were stoked.

They actually wanted to hang out with us!?

Definitely in.

When we got there – some of their friends were there. We walked up to the group, and they let us stand around and hang out too.

We felt cool.

Bored- but cool.

They were actually talking to us and treating us like people instead of annoying little siblings that they wanted to go away forever.

We were soaking it up.

But then, they were just standing around. Some of our friends had shown up and were playing.

We glanced at each other and slowly slipped out of the circle and moved towards our friends.

The older kids didn't seem to mind one bit.

We went over to the double swings where our friends were.

We were having the time of our lives- spinning each other so high on the double swing trying to make each other throw up.

I was up in the air, and I noticed a car whip up next to the park- and a guy got out and started yelling.

I was spinning so fast at this point I couldn't even see what was happening.

I yelled out Banana or whatever the code word was that day- so that I could start spinning my way back down to the ground.

By the time I got down – the guy was getting back into his car.

My brother, cousin and their friends looked like they were ready to fight him.

He said- I'll be back, and you'll be sorry.

And then he took off.

We were rattled.

My brother and my cousin went back to the house and said that they would be right back. When my cousin came back- my brother wasn't with him.

He had left with his friends to handle it. My cousin told us that we didn't have to worry and that he would play capture the flag with us AND jailbreak if we didn't tell our parents about what happened.

He assured us that it was nothing. Just a stupid argument.

Listen,

He never played with us anymore.

He was elite level good, so he made everyone step up their game.

He made it more fun.

When he said that all we had to do was not tell?!

It wasn't even a hard choice for us then.

What guy?

Let's play!

It was just about to start getting dark out and everyone we had been waiting for had arrived.

It was a perfect night.

We kicked off with capture the flag until it was dark enough to make jailbreak really fun.

The harder it is to see- the easier it is to hide- *obviously*.

In jailbreak- you are either finding the prisoners and locking them up- or hiding and trying to rush to the jail to break everyone free without getting caught.

No matter what side you are on-

You are either hiding, holding your breath, creeping around, or running full force.

All of your senses go into overdrive in the dark.

I loved it.

I absolutely loved it.

It was finally dark enough for my favorite game to start.

Everybody ran to hide.

I was moving around trying to see the jail.

Had anyone been caught yet?

Did I need to try and break anyone free?

I was sneaking around trying to find a new hiding spot when I saw my older cousin hiding by the bushes.

He didn't see me- which was weird because, like I said- he was elite level good at this game.

Yet here he was- in an obvious hiding spot – not even paying attention.

Had he lost his touch?

He was looking at something- so I followed his gaze.

I immediately felt sick.

I saw what he was looking at.

A man was walking up to the park.

Something wasn't right.

My body was screaming at me to get everyone out of there quietly and immediately.

My cousin looked over and saw me and told me to be quiet and stay here.

I listened.

I was terrified.

I was looking around for my other cousins- for my friends.

Everything felt crystal clear. It didn't even feel as dark anymore. I could see a lot of them hiding.

Nobody saw this man walking up.

I remember praying- please please *please* – don't let them move. Just freeze everyone for a minute until this guy is gone.

The guy!

I was so busy looking for my friends that I wasn't watching the guy.

I didn't know why I had such a terrible feeling, but it was there- and I was listening.

I was always right about my feelings so far.

I looked back and I saw him walking over towards a tree in the park and he got down on his hands and knees.

It was so strange to see.

My brain didn't quite understand what was happening.

I had full body chills.

This wasn't right.

I watched him as he crawled behind the tree and laid down on his stomach- arms crossed-

Army crawl ready.

I realized that if I hadn't watched him with my own eyes- I wouldn't have even know he was there.

I couldn't sit here and hide.

What was he doing?

This made no sense.

I was terrified.

Something awful was about to happen.

I could feel it.

My cousin must have felt the same thing- because he stepped out of the bushes and started yelling-

"Hey! Who are you!?"

"Hey!

WHO?

ARE?

YOU?"

"Answer me!"

This made me feel brave.

We could take this guy out together!

I yelled out-

"Yeah! And why are you laying behind the tree!?"

Mainly because, I really wanted to know. I was hopeful it was a good explanation. I could laugh and be like oh my gosh – I never even thought about that!

But, I knew that, as much as I wanted one- there wasn't a good explanation.

And then it got even more weird.

He wouldn't answer us.

He tried to not move- like maybe we didn't really see him.

We kept yelling who are you- what are you doing- what do you want?

We shouted out that we were playing a game and that there were a lot of us here.

We were demanding for him to tell us who he was and what he wanted- walking slowly closer to the tree.

Nothing.

No response.

Some of the older kids started coming out to see what we were yelling about.

We pointed to the tree, and all started closing in on him.

I had a good angle and I saw him slowly slide his body up the trunk of the tree. He was trying to stay hidden behind it.

It looked like he reached for something.

Alarm bells were shooting off.

We had to stop getting closer to this guy.

I told my cousin- but he wasn't listening.

Him and the other kids kept moving forward.

I had to get the adults immediately.

I felt it with every single part of my soul.

I took off – sprinting towards the house.

I burst through the door – completely out of breath, saying "The man! The man! There's a man – behind the tree. I don't know why he's there or who he is!"

I completely shocked our parents. They immediately responded with - whoa- whoa- whoa – slow down.

They wanted me to start at the beginning.

They needed all the information.

Of course, they did- but I also didn't have time for that.

I also knew that I didn't have any option.

They needed to know how serious this was so that they could help me help everyone.

As quickly as they would let me- I told them the story and as soon as I was done- my older cousin ran in through the door and he said everything was fine- it was just one of the neighborhood kids messing around.

It was scary- but it was just a joke.

I had over exaggerated.

I knew he was lying.

But the look he gave me- I knew I needed to pretend I believed him for a minute.

Now *I* needed more information.

He grabbed my hand and walked me out the door. The minute we got outside he said that my cousin- the one that was the same age as me- was in trouble and we had to hurry.

He'd tell me more back at the park.

We ran full speed.

When we got there- we hid again.

But this time, when we were hiding – we were watching a man yell at my cousin while he was sitting on the street corner under the light.

Who was this guy?

Why was he so mad?

How could we get to him?

My sweet- wonderful- innocent cousin.

Through his tears- he kept saying that he was just playing and that his wrists hurt.

That was when I realized -he had his hands behind his back.

I felt like I was back in that classroom in 4th grade.

Why were his hands behind his back?

Why wasn't he moving them?

He had handcuffs on.

Why did this man have him in handcuffs!?

I watched him walk away from my cousin and walk down the street. We were waiting to see what he was going to do next when he disappeared out of our sight.

We were going to run over and grab him and get the heck out of there. We crept forward getting as close as we could- when we saw a police car pulling up.

I remember breathing a heavy sigh of relief.

The calvary was here to save the day!

The same man got out of the car, and we saw him put his shirt back on.

His official police uniform.

He didn't want us to know he was an officer when he entered the park?

My brain was scrambling to make this make sense.

He started yelling at my cousin again.

My cousin was crying harder - trying to tell him that he was just playing a game. He wasn't doing anything wrong. Please, he just wanted to go home.

He wouldn't listen to my cousin.

He didn't believe him.

My older cousin and I looked at each other and I knew we were both realizing what this really meant.

This man was a police officer.

A police officer who had a little kid in handcuffs?

A police officer who not only did not announce who he was- but also, wouldn't tell us when we asked over and over?

The man that scared me to my core and sent me running so fast out of the park to get help- was an adult, male police officer?

This was who we could go to for anything?

I heard my cousin start to beg him to please loosen the handcuffs. His arms and his wrists were really hurting.

He was begging him through his sobs.

He wouldn't. He wouldn't loosen them. He wouldn't take them off. He just left him there on the curb and walked back to his car.

Nope.

Nope.

Nope.

Every single thing felt wrong.

I felt like everything I had been taught didn't matter anymore.

I only knew one thing.

I had to get our parents.

I knew I needed more information so I asked my cousin to tell me, as fast as he possibly could- everything that had happened from the time I left.

He said that the guy never said who he was – just tried to keep hiding behind the tree until they walked up and started asking him who he was.

He said he was nobody and told them to leave him alone.

He started walking over to the church.

Everyone followed at a distance.

My other cousins were hiding over there.

We always hid all over the church grounds.

It was under construction- so nobody was using it at night.

The man found my cousin and pulled him out of his hiding spot under the tool trailer and had immediately pinned him down and cuffed him.

He moved him out to the curb under the streetlight. They didn't realize that it was a police officer until I was back.

Suddenly- it hit me.

Nobody knew who he was.

That meant that he didn't identify himself as an officer when he was pulling my cousin out from under the trailer.

When he was slapping the cuffs on his wrists.

I knew right then and there that those tears - were fear.

My cousin had thought it was the man that had yelled at all of us when I was on the double swing.

I was so angry.

The kids had all been yelling at him. Asking what he was doing- why he was cuffing our friend. They all shouted over and over that we were playing jailbreak.

Nobody was doing anything wrong.

But he wasn't listening.

That's when my older cousin left to run home and get me.

I nodded and told him I was going back to the house to get our parents while he kept an eye on what was happening.

I ran back and told our parents that they had to come to the park.

My aunt was up and ready to run out the door the second I told her he was handcuffed and crying.

Right as she went to walk out the door- there was a knock.

She was FUMING. She wanted answers- and she wanted them now.

She was going to get them.

My aunt opened the door and there was the officer and my cousin.

He ran into the house, and she grabbed him and hugged him to her side.

The officer started saying that my cousin was seen breaking into the construction site and that we were lucky that they were letting him go with just a warning.

He told my aunt and uncle that they should really have a talk with him about how serious this is.

What he didn't know -

Was that my aunt already knew everything.

She caught him off guard, asking him- did you handcuff my son?

He looked her dead in the face and said that he did not.

I couldn't believe it.

Not only did he scare us all- ruin our perfect night- ruin jailbreak- try to arrest my cousin, but now- now he was lying on top of it?

Officers were supposed to be seekers of justice.

The epitome of truth!

But he was lying.

I knew he was.

I saw it with my own eyes!

I didn't understand how he could be saying this.

And then she grabbed me and pulled me forward right in between them and said- "Then why did my niece just run back here in tears terrified - saying some man had crept into the park and got onto his hands and knees and tried to hide behind a tree? A man who would not identify himself even when they asked repeatedly?"

Then she grabbed my cousins' arm and held up his hand.

I didn't even see it until then.

The marks.

He had angry, deep red marks on both of his wrists.

"And these marks?

Please tell me how these got on my sons' wrist if you didn't cuff him?

Do you know how serious lying to me is?

What is your boss's number?

Never mind- I have it."

And she shut the door in his face.

Believe me when I say, she called.

And *believe* me when I say -she talked.

We all did.

And sharing an experience like that- is more powerful than people realize.

Police officers and teachers weren't all they were cracked up to be.

I didn't idolize them anymore.

I didn't want to grow up and be either of them anymore.

The only lesson that I learned that day- was that safe people weren't really safe after all.

The next week at school we were introduced to the D.A.R.E program.

Let me tell you that- in the 90's, our teachers were hyping us UP about this program.

Everything in the 90's was all about D.A.R.E.

We had commercials- news stories- shows- everything was about how great D.A.R.E was.

We were really excited to hear that it was our time!

We were getting an entire class period learning from a police officer!

I was sure that he could restore some of our faith in the law that had been ripped away from us.

I was hopeful.

Maybe it wasn't all of them.

Maybe it was just one of them.

Our teacher told us that he was here, so we all needed to take our seats and get ready.

We were PUMPED!

Swinging our feet- moving around – anxious to see what an awesome day this was going to be.

And then he walked in.

The officer that arrested my cousin.

He came in friendly- ready to teach!

As he introduced himself and looked around the room he saw me- and his face fell.

He quickly started to scan the room and found my cousin.

He stopped talking.

Just staring – not sure what to do.

Then said something about an emergency.

He'd reschedule.

Sorry kids! I'll be back!

Another lie.

He walked out the door and that was it.

Goodbye super awesome D.A.R.E experience.

Elementary was over.

Good riddance.

We were off to a new school.

Jr. High was good, honestly.

I kept being funny and we had a ton of new kids to meet.

New school. New teachers. New classes.

My Jr. High math teachers were both great. I still couldn't manage to make the majority of it stick- but somehow I did just well enough to skate by.

I also cheated.

A lot.

And I got a lot of "help" with my homework.

Nobody seemed to care though.

As long as I looked like I was doing good- and I was doing great everywhere else- nobody cared.

I didn't make waves.

I was funny – but I was compliant.

It worked.

I rode that for two years.

I helped teachers with their classrooms.

I made people laugh.

I had a solid group of friends.

Life should have been great.

But I still wasn't okay.

And each year- things were getting more complicated.

I was still feeling like I wasn't ready to grow up.

I didn't want to.

There was still a lot of drama- a lot of mean- a lot of bad around growing up.

Everyone wanted to start dating, drinking, smoking.

It was starting to feel like everyone wanted to grow up but me.

My brother is 5 years older than me.

I knew all of his friends.

When they started wanting me to hang out with them- I was so excited that I would have pretty much done anything.

When they asked me if I wanted to get drunk- I was in. When they asked me if I wanted to get high- I was in.

I remember feeling so cool.

One time- a group of older girls offered me a ride home.

They were heading to my house to see my brother and his friends.

The only catch was that we were smoking weed on the way there.

I said cool and they lit a blunt.

I smoked the entire thing with them.

I had smoked one time before this.

They kept asking me if I wanted to put it out and I said no. I'm good when you're good.

They laughed.

They thought that I was going to regret it.

They thought I'd be a mess.

But I was fine.

They were losing their minds over how much weed I could smoke.

Where was the award for that!?

I honestly felt like I was just really good at smoking weed.

They said that I could hang out with them any time after that.

I thought, cool! That was easy.

High school would be a breeze.

I had been around it enough with my brother and his friends. And honestly- I liked it better than anything else I knew about.

Everyone I was around was nice when they smoked.

My skin wasn't burning and on fire when I smoked.

We talked about everything when we smoked.

It never felt scary to me.

So, when anyone offered, of course I was in.

It felt like a fun, wonderful place to be. The older kids loved me. I felt like I belonged. I felt like oh! It was just that I am ahead of my time.

I have found my people.

Even my brother was nice to me when we were smoking.

It didn't take long for this to turn into all that I did.

I burnt out fast and didn't want to do it anymore.

I was tired all the time.

I wasn't sleeping because my brothers' friends would want me to sneak out when my parents went to bed. We would hang out all night talking and smoking.

It was so fun at first but then – it was the same things- the same conversations – the same people- the same music.

My friends all wanted me to bring them- get them things- bring stuff to parties.

I just wanted people to want me to be there.

I hated the pressure.

I was tired.

I needed to sleep.

This wasn't fun anymore.

I was spent.

The more tired I got- the more guilty I started to feel.

Sneaking around- omitting information –not following the law…

My parents didn't deserve that.

My parents didn't deserve what we would put them through if we got caught, either.

And- we hadn't gotten caught. I should get out while I was ahead, right?

My parents always encouraged me to be me.

None of this – felt like me.

I knew that I could tell them everything- that they could help me fix everything.

But- I also knew that I couldn't tell them without changing everything.

I couldn't picture a world where everything got better if I told.

There would be fighting. A lot of people would get in trouble. A lot of people would question every single thing anyone said. We would all have to tell our stories. Some would be too scared. Some would tell more – some would sound like me.

Everyone in the whole district would know.

Everyone would know I told.

And if by any chance the teachers got away with it- like if nobody would talk?

People would think I lied.

I never lie. I will find truth and make it work to my advantage- sure. But I don't lie.

The thought that people would think I did... that made me not want to tell ever.

And what if my very first mean teacher got away with it?

She would be even worse.

Maybe this wasn't so bad. Maybe it was the lesser of two evils. Everyone else was making it through okay. They weren't telling or getting anyone else involved.

I just needed to hang in there.

Besides- the police officer was still on the force. Moving right on up in his career.

Maybe the bad guys always won.

I let my experiences lead the way and I kept my mouth shut.

I filled my life with more things to do.

I thought I could distract myself away from all of it.

I joined the cheerleading squad and dove more into softball.

I loved to act annoyed while saying my new catchphrase: "Sorry, I can't I have practice."

I wasn't annoyed.

This was all intentional.

I wanted better things.

I wanted a better life.

I wanted my life back.

Before all of this.

I was determined to get it back.

But I thought that I still needed excuses and I wasn't confident in my decision to get my life back on track because I was afraid.

What if I lost all of my friends?

What if it was worse?

What if I was too far behind? What if it was too late?

It was scary.

But it was working.

So, I kept moving forward.

I was doing really well. I was still having fun with my friends but not hanging out as much outside of school.

I was feeling good.

I was really enjoying sports and even started to love school again.

My teachers were good. I was in good graces with all of them- even the ones that everyone thought were awful.

I thought they were great.

The hardest thing was the hives.

I couldn't get rid of them.

They were getting worse.

But - I was managing.

Things could always be worse, right?

One day I was on my way to class when one of my favorite teachers asked me to pop in quick and chat with her.

I gladly followed her into the classroom, but immediately wondered why.

She never asked me to come talk to her.

And I was going to be late for class...

I'm sure she'd write me a pass.

It'll be fine.

Relax.

I walked in and was shocked.

There was a circle of chairs – with almost all of my teachers standing next to them.

There was one chair left.

My first thought was-

Omg are they surprising me to tell me how much I have improved?

Have they noticed how hard I have been working?

Am I getting an award!?

I didn't know what else it could possibly be.

The room felt weird, but I didn't know to be alarmed.

I had never experienced anything like this in my life until now.

I walked in and when I reached the chair- we all sat down.

I noticed it then.

The position of the chair was weird.

I had my back to the wall and was facing the door.

It felt like they were all around me.

I looked around the room at all the somber faces.

I was not getting an award.

I didn't know why I was here- but I knew it wasn't good.

I didn't do anything wrong.

Suddenly- I felt like I was suffocating.

I started sweating.

I started breaking out in hives.

I closed my eyes.

I barely even heard the words.

They overheard someone talking about parties and they knew I was involved– that my brother and his friends- and a lot of my friends were involved.

People were watching us.

The police.

The school.

They had proof.

They were so disappointed in me.

I wanted to laugh.

I wanted to cry.

I wanted to start jumping up and down - screaming – throw my arms around.

I felt like I was losing my mind.

I couldn't believe that all my hard work - was for nothing.

Busting my ass to change my life- saying no to everyone.

My friends, my brother, my brothers' friends- everyone.

I turned down everything.

I was FIGHTING for the life I wanted- I was spending so many frustrating hours trying to make math stick in my brain – and this?!

This.

This is what they noticed.

What my brother was doing.

What my friends were doing.

What the friends of my brother- were doing.

What the kids that were partying were doing.

Nothing about me.

None of them knew me.

After all the hours I spent helping- learning- trying-

participating – practicing – studying.

This is what they saw.

Everyone. And Everything. But. Me.

And just like that-

I was gone.

I don't remember anything that was said.

I was out of my body again.

I was floating.

I was watching.

This time was different though. I had been here before.

I was aware that I wasn't in my body.

And this time- as I watched a room full of adults ganging up on me – I realized- I don't have to take this. I don't have to sit here and listen to this.

They don't have proof.

I wasn't doing anything that they said.

I needed to get out of here and stop letting these "adults" think that this was okay.

And- even if I had been partying still- making me feel like a piece of shit was not the way to make me want to do better.

I felt it happening. Like the moment just before the rollercoaster ride really starts. You hear the click and feel it slightly move.

You take a big breath.

And you know everything is about to move really fast.

You hold on.

And then- you take off.

I was back.

I was sitting in the chair.

I looked down at my hands.

Sweaty- scared little fists.

I looked around the room.

They were saying how bad I was- how disappointed they were- how they expected more from me. What a loser I was being. How if this is what I wanted- I'd never be anything- just a loser, drug addict, alcoholic.

They took turns tearing me down for things I wasn't doing.

Trying to scare me into being good.

Trying to scare me into telling them things.

What was even happening?

How was this my life no matter what I did?

At one point- I let out a shocked laugh and asked if they had me confused with someone else.

I genuinely thought that they had to have me confused with someone else.

They looked around and I realized – they weren't really sure.

ALL OF THIS AND THEY WERENT EVEN REALLY SURE!

They said they had a pretty good idea that it was me.

A.

Pretty.

Good.

Idea.

I told them it wasn't me. I told them that I wasn't doing any of that. I didn't know anything about a party. I had been at practice.

Ask!

I had an alibi!

They looked at each other and then said that they wouldn't be asking anyone.

They knew it was me.

But...

The just admitted that they didn't?

And- I really did have an alibi.

They didn't care.

They had already made up their minds that I was bad.

All of the hard work meant nothing.

My character – meant nothing.

My actions- meant nothing.

Then they made it extra special.

They wanted to make sure I'd never forget this moment.

They told me that I wasn't allowed to go on the bus trip to see the Chicago Cubs baseball game for the end of the year, because of my terrible behavior.

I saw red.

For the first time in my life- I saw red.

I had never been so angry in my entire life.

I took those tiny balled up sweaty fists and I squeezed even harder.

I stood up.

I wanted to say something clever, but I knew that if I opened my mouth- the tears would fall.

I would lose control.

I would fall apart.

I just had an entire group of people that I loved, that I respected, that I wanted to be around, to learn from… judge me without ever even getting to know me.

That was the thing too- I really thought that they did.

I thought that they really saw me.

I thought that we understood each other- respected each other.

Turns out- that was a one-way street. I felt like the rug was pulled out from under me again.

I squeezed even harder.

I would not cry.

There was no way I was falling apart, not now.

There was no way that I was letting them win.

One of my teachers was a big, grumpy – mean older man that everyone feared. Up until this moment- I thought he was great.

I thought he was great until I walked into this room and found him there.

He told me in a loud – booming voice to sit down in my seat RIGHT NOW.

He told me that my disrespectful behavior would not be tolerated.

That he would not tolerate me.

I locked eyes with him and didn't budge.

He stood up to challenge me.

I am 5 ft as an adult. He would tower over me now. He definitely towered over me then.

I did what any tiny person would do when a giant man challenges you with his stature.

I laughed.

Not because it was funny but because the fact that he thought that he could threaten me with his body was so wrong that it was comically bad.

I couldn't believe this was happening.

Right then and there- I decided.

I wouldn't tolerate them.

I would never tolerate this bullshit again.

Nobody was going to treat me like this, ever again.

Nobody was keeping me from anything.

Shoulders back.

Head up.

I looked straight ahead, and I started walking toward the door.

As soon as I was out of the circle of chairs- I could breathe again.

I was almost to the door when I realized-

They aren't stopping me.

They can't stop me.

They do not have ANYTHING on me.

If they did- they wouldn't have let me leave. My parents would be here. The principal would be here. They did this on their own. They weren't supposed to be doing this. They knew they weren't supposed to be doing this.

I looked back with one hand on the door handle and with the strongest face I could show- I said:

"I'm going on that bus trip. If you have a problem, call my parents and we'll tell them about this."

And I walked out.

Head held high.

Shoulders back.

I walked out of the room- and immediately to the bathroom.

I waited and I waited.

None of them followed me.

Everyone was in class.

I cried.

I sobbed.

I wept with my entire body.

I should have felt great.

It should have felt like a win.

I stood up to the bullies!

But- it didn't feel good.

This time, I didn't want to keep working hard.

This time, I just wanted to say fuck it.

Fuck everything.

Fuck everyone.

Fuck it.

I'm done.

I was catapulted back to 4th grade. Losing myself. Losing my faith. Losing my feelings.

I couldn't feel things the same way anymore.

I wasn't hopeful in the same way.

I didn't have a safe space at school.

Now I didn't even feel like I had teachers.

I didn't care anymore.

Weed and alcohol for everyone.

When I stopped crying – I started to pull myself together.

I thought- if everyone already assumes that I am loser, that I'd never be anything- that I was just an alcoholic- a drug addict- a party girl on the road to nowhere. I'd prove them wrong.

I'd be the best one there was.

And I'd have fun doing it.

Who even cared what happened anymore?

Nothing good was coming for me from school.

That was apparent.

I was going to be judged for this no matter what- I already was, so, I may as well do it on my terms right?

It was fun when I was letting it be fun.

It was the over thinking- it was the fear of getting in trouble.

I mean, obviously I didn't have to be worried about that.

I was getting "caught" even when I wasn't doing anything.

Fuck it.

I was diving in headfirst.

They never called my parents.

I went on the trip.

It ended up raining for hours while we waited to see if it would break.

It didn't.

The game was cancelled.

We got back on the bus and headed home.

It is poetic– if you think about it - and I wouldn't change it for the world.

I still played in the rain.

I still laughed with my friends.

Wrigley stadium played music and we danced in the rain.

Those teachers had to chaperone and let me be on the bus.

They didn't break me.

They wounded me.

But I healed stronger.

None of this should have happened.

This story doesn't end exactly like the last one, and that is okay.

Everything that happened set me up for a lot of shitty things that happened throughout the rest of my life.

I used to dream about what my life would have been like if I didn't have these terrible teachers.

If teachers like my favorite one filled my life instead of becoming my one lifeline.

That isn't what happened though.

And that's okay because life is what you make it, and I was determined to make it something good.

It gave me a lot of really cool lessons.

Here are some of my favorites.

It is not your job to worry about what happens.

A lot of us- spend a lot of time- worrying about or making excuses for -the actions of others.

We make excuses for them for a lot of different reasons. In these stories- it was because I couldn't make sense of why someone would do these things.

It made me feel like I had to be missing something big.

And as curious creatures- we want to know why.

Why would someone do this?

But a lot of times- our need to know why- puts us in the line of fire.

Just like it did to me – time and time again.

But I had to know why.

I would face the fire.

I made excuses when I didn't have enough information for why.

A lot of the reason that I didn't want to tell or get help was honestly because as bad as it was- I didn't want to get anyone in trouble.

Not the teachers.

Not my brother.

Not my friends.

Not his friends.

I felt like maybe this was all a misunderstanding.

Seriously- what if I just didn't have enough info.

Maybe there were things I didn't know.

Maybe nobody would take me seriously.

Maybe my teachers would be meaner to me.

Maybe she would be meaner to all of us.

There was a lot that I didn't know. There was a lot that I didn't understand.

And listen- I had never been in these situations before.

I didn't have anything to base this experience off of.

When it all started-

I was just a 4th grader- winging it.

I thought that the whole world was made of magic, and I just wanted to hear more Tom Petty songs.

I had no idea that there was so much more to the world.

That there is bad shit everywhere.

But

You cannot change that.

You cannot make the whole world be what you want.

Worrying about it and stressing over it- will not change it.

You cannot make people be better.

No matter how much *you* want it.

And it is not your responsibility to make them- or want it for them.

When people act in a way that harms you- or others– shout it out if you want to!

Tell anyone that you want.

Get help.

Whatever you have to do to make it stop happening to you- to others.

Stand up for what is right.

I should have screamed in that hallway the minute I saw her leaning over the chair.

I should have run to get someone.

I should have done ANYTHING that involved an adult – every single time – I felt scared around another adult.

I should have told anyone who would listen to me. And I should have told over and over and over again until someone did something.

I definitely should have told my parents.

I should have let them make a scene.

I should have let everyone get involved.

What would have happened?

Maybe she would have hit me hard enough to leave a mark and at least then- I would have had some proof.

Bottom line-

You aren't responsible for their actions.

Tell.

And if the first person can't help you- or doesn't help you- tell someone else.

Keep talking until someone helps you!

And-

Do not be afraid to tell.

If they get in trouble- that's not on you.

Why?

I'm glad you asked.

OWN YOUR ACTIONS.

If you don't want to get in trouble- don't do things that get you in trouble.

Seriously.

That simple.

If you don't do things that you can get in trouble for- you never have to worry.

Seems easy enough right?

Why is this a lesson?

Well because, apparently- it's not.

There are a whole lot of people out here doing things that they aren't proud of. The don't want people to know. Things that they hide away.

I say- if it doesn't sit well with your soul- don't do it.

You have to be confident in your actions.

It's as easy as that.

And if you do things that don't sit well with your soul- well, at least own up when you get caught.

It's easy thinking about it like that, right?

Well- it's the same thing on the flip side.

If someone does something to you that they don't want anyone to know about?

They shouldn't have done it then.

It is not your problem.

Tell anyone you want.

Do what you want with it.

It's your story.

The minute that they acted towards you- involved you- it became your story.

Nobody can tell you what to do with that.

The more you put yourself first- the better your story gets.

It is not your responsibility to hide things for other people.

The actions of others- is not yours to figure out.

How you respond to it- is all that is on you.

Kids should not fix adult situations.

Ever.

Yet- it happens more than we realize.

What I have learned along the way- is that talking to kids like they are people -is where it's at.

Kids need adults who hear them.

Who let them dream.

Who teach them how to be even more of themselves.

If you are bitter- stay away from kids.

If you have a short fuse- get irritated with questions- feel like life has killed your soul- please, stay away from kids.

We assume because they are tiny little humans that they are fine – they are just playing and learning and living life.

But kids? Kids don't know how to say- "Hi! I think that I am starting to feel anxious because my teacher is really scary without that becoming a really big deal."

Kids don't know how to tell you that they are picking up on your energy- on your words- on your tone- and learning how to act based on those cues.

We obviously cannot be perfect around kids but when we aren't- we need to be better about explaining what is happening. Why we are feeling how we are.

They know so much more than we give them credit for.

When we let kids be kids while also getting to know them as people – it changes things.

While we should never have them fixing things- or being involved directly in hot spots, talking to them shows them that the world isn't perfect.

When we talk to them about why we had a big reaction- or why we were upset – or why we were stressed- it helps them understand feelings. Theirs and others.

Remember- things that seem obvious to us- aren't always. They are learning- and you can't know something- until you know it!

Even the easiest things- we had to learn at some point.

I know adults that struggle with communicating feelings.

How do we expect kids to?

Talking to your kids like people. Real people. Asking them questions- answering theirs.

Getting curious when you don't know.

And if they ever tell you that they are afraid of someone they shouldn't be- tread lightly and listen more than you speak.

Stay calm- no matter how hard that may be.

And most of all- no matter what is happening, just be there.

Sometimes- even if they keep you in the dark the way that I did to my parents- just being there - just being a loving home- that helped me substantially.

That gave me the courage to get through it.

It gave me a place to breathe.

Be a safe space for them- because this world… this world isn't going to show them that all the time no matter how great of a job you do.

You can't change it.

Listen- this story doesn't end with me saying- I am so grateful for these terrible teachers. I'm stronger- better- I figured it all out right then and there and everything was great.

In fact, it was the opposite. If you keep reading- you'll know that this took me to some really awful places.

But it also took me to some beautiful ones- and I came out stronger.

I heal.

I find myself.

I keep finding myself.

The journey unfolds.

But- it happened.

And I still to this day can't say that life was better because of it.

And I have seen my friends that went through it too- and if I were a betting gal (which, I only am sometimes) I would bet that they would tell you that they are most definitely not better because of it.

But that's the thing.

Not everything that happens is designed to make you better.

Not everything unfolds and feels like magic.

Some things happen because shitty things do happen- and we need to be aware of them.

Some things happen because some people- they don't want to change.

Ever.

We need to be aware of that too- because we are not in charge of other people's actions right?

We are not in charge of their lives.

We do not get a say in what they do while they are here- no matter how badly we want to.

I don't want these mean ass old ladies to be mean ass old ladies.

I would love for them to have found peace- made amends with their own traumas.

I know that anyone that behaves that way has a world of trauma locked inside of them.

They wouldn't act that way if they didn't.

So- I feel for them.

I empathize that – they are old mean ladies- and that they are still old mean ladies and that makes me see them differently.

It makes me see that it isn't really them- its trauma.

It's passed down.

They couldn't escape it.

I hope that their kids do.

I can't image what life was like growing up with that at school and at home.

And that makes me grateful that I didn't.

*There is gratitude in everything.

There is understanding in everything.

There is peace in everything.*

No matter what happens in life- we can find something to connect it with that feels peaceful to us.

We can find peace in anything- as unbelievable as that may be to some to imagine.

In some situations- it is a lot harder to find than others.

For me- all of these stories that I share- were pretty hard to sort through.

But- that's why I share them.

I am proof that if you really want to live your life as peacefully as possible- you can- once you learn to trust in this lesson.

And that?

That is a hard fact to lean into sometimes.

I've wanted to fight it a lot too.

I am hopeful that in sharing some of these- you can see it. You can feel it. You can relate it back to your own story- however that looks to you.

In this one- I really had to break it down and think about what would cause a person to do that to another person and it broke my heart.

I can't imagine carrying around that kind of pain – that kind of hurt- for a lifetime and never getting to actually enjoy your time here.

That realization was what made me able to let it go - to make peace

- because -

I didn't want to carry this around with me anymore.

In writing this story – I realized a lot.

I did what I felt was right.

I made it through.

I am healing every day and it taught me a lot about what I didn't want my life to look like.

It taught me a lot of lessons quickly- so that now- I have a whole lot of life left to live in a big, beautiful way.

I will be forever grateful for that. I will forever have peace in that.

When we make peace- we can let it go.

Accepting – healing – and letting go- that is how we move forward. We grow.

We change the world a little less trauma at a time.

We have to stick up for ourselves.

A lot of us don't.

And a lot of us look for people who will do it for us.

I did because of things like this.

I thought that someone sticking up for me – was love. Someone not letting another person hurt me was love. And- I wasn't wrong. It is a form of love.

I love my friends- my family.

I will stick up for them and they will stick up for me. But when we spend all our time sticking up for people- and they never have to do it for themselves?

They aren't learning that tool.

We have to let people defend themselves as well.

We have to let people figure out how to best solve their problems.

always doing it for them – if someone is always doing it for us- it's a disservice.

We all have our own ways of handling things- and if you never learn yours- if you keep jumping in for someone else- how do we figure out what that unique way is?

We have to be able to stick up for ourselves.

It is powerful.

It connects you- to you.

We tend to put ourselves last, though, because we don't really know how, and it doesn't really feel right when you grow up confused about big situations- like I did in this story.

No matter how shitty something in your past is- it happened, and for reasons unknown to us- it needed to happen.

When we find the lesson in it- we heal.

When we share our story– we leave others feeling less alone.

Not feel so lost.

And we go through it head on.

We process.

We heal.

Some things happen to us because we need to feel them all the way through. We need to know that this is something that we need to help change.

This is part of our story that needs to come out so that other things can happen.

Maybe you read this story and you are the one that runs with it.

Maybe this story fed your soul, and it starts to fuel you towards a positive change.

An idea.

Who knows!

That is the fun part.

That is the unknown.

That is not for me to figure out.

I just know that this story is my story for a reason-

and if I share it with you- and you run with it?

Or if it helps you heal?

If it helps you share yours?

Sparks you in some way?

All. Worth. it.

Nothing meant for you will miss you.

Me being pulled to write and share this specific story

means that somewhere- someone needs it.

I needed it when I was little.

Maybe – if I had gotten my hands on a story like

this- I would have told.

Maybe I would have just said hey- read this book- I understand it too much and I need help.

Who knows?!

Again, this is the fun part.

The minute you let yourself feel it- really feel it- sink into it, you will realize that the trauma you have been lessening- because "it could have been worse" is becoming worse.

It's becoming worse because you won't recognize it. You won't let it out.

That energy needs somewhere to go.

When it doesn't have anywhere to go it sits on our body. That can look like anything- like hives, nervous habits, physical pain- weight – mental health – ANYTHING.

But until we recognize our trauma for what it was for us- and only for us, we will carry it in an unhealthy way.

Even if you are managing- life isn't what it should be yet.

It can't be.

Because life needs you to…

Let that shit go and shake that shit out.

Trauma will happen.

It's not always deserved.

It's not always a big karmic lesson.

Sometimes- it just sucks.

Sometimes you get pulled into other people's stuff.

Sometimes the answer is that people aren't perfect.

Some aren't dealing with their trauma, and they are projectile vomiting their trauma onto others – and not everyone is going to heal.

Not everyone gets it right quickly.

And sometimes we still mess up when we are trying to do better.

Our trauma can pass onto others.

We can inflict new trauma onto others.

That is why it is so important that we heal.

That we recognize it for what it really did to us.

Once we do – we can find out what it can do for us.

We use it.

We let it go and find some peace within ourselves.

We forgive ourselves for not speaking up- for not doing things differently- for all the hard years that came after it.

We start to forgive ourselves for everything because it all came from somewhere- and here we are, acknowledging it. Really trying our best to move forward and use our situations that hurt us the most, for good.

Ease up on yourself.

Bad people don't worry about getting better.

If you are making baby steps- celebrate. You are good. You are trying. And even if you haven't always been good- we can always be better.

We can always heal more.

I am not the first person to have a shitty teacher, or a shitty boss.

In fact – every single story that you read from me- I am not the first.

I am not the last.

That is why we bond together. We mend and we form a healthy alliance.

We vow to put ourselves first and take no shit from this world.

This is where we really learn about our value.

We are not too soft for this world.

This world needs us.

REALLY needs us to be our most authentic selves.

It needs us to bring our light- our good- our uniqueness into the world to inspire others to find theirs.

Imagine if every truly wonderful person you know had millions and millions of dollars in their bank account from doing something that they loved- feeling lighter than ever- more inspiring than ever.

I think of a world FULL of my favorite teachers.

The lifelines.

The more of us there are- the less shit there is.

It is literally up to us to shake the shit out of the world by being ourselves.

By not quitting.

By not listening to the people that don't even matter!

We deserve great things.

We would do incredible things with our money- our time – our power.

We want more of our people with resources putting their greatness into the world.

That is where change starts!

*Don't let anyone take away your trip to a Cubs game.

In fact-

Don't let anyone take anything away from you, ever again.

Period. Point Blank.*

Sometimes – making waves- catches you in one.

When I think about this story, and how it all started- the only way to change it is if I would have left my friend in that classroom. I would have left him all alone. I would have knowingly – left him all alone. I can't imagine what else would have happened had I left.

Sure – maybe I wouldn't have had my whole shitshow of a story- but, maybe I would have had a worse story.

Leaving my friend- felt wrong in every single way.

I don't know the person that doesn't bust into a room to save someone.

That's not me.

I felt a force – bigger than me- screaming to stay.

Screaming that this wasn't right.

Screaming at me to listen.

It physically moved my body into the storm.

I would never choose another option.

And guess what- maybe it made my story harder- but - I handled every single thing that came my way.

I never had to regret my actions.

And now because I did bust in that day-

I have such a deeper understanding and appreciation of my entire life going through this process and writing these stories.

I realized- I wouldn't change it.

I wasn't supposed to become whoever that girl was.

It was always this.

I mourned the loss of that girl a long time ago,

thinking that she was gone forever.

But in writing this- I found that she was always here.

She was just hiding.

Letting me build.

Letting me figure it out.

She is here now.

And let me tell you-

She is fierce.

She stays standing in any storm.

She calms the storm.

And sometimes- she is the storm.

I am proud of myself. For making it through, for facing my fears, for acknowledging this part of my life and for letting the hives go.

I saw my 5th and 6th grade math teachers together a few years ago when I was out with my mom. They were having a garage sale and they barely remembered who I was.

When I told them- they immediately remembered my class and asked me for gossip about some of them.

Not good gossip like who is successful- who loves their life?!

They wanted to know the negative things about everyone.

It was like they never left.

I looked at them - I looked down at the table with all their cheap crap everywhere and realized, this?

This is who I let make me feel so afraid?

So bad about myself?

These two mean old ladies with all their weird knick-knacks which- most of- belonged in the trash?

These two old ladies that were still stuck in Elementary school?

My mom knows everything now.

She was appreciating this moment as much as I was.

I said that my entire class was doing incredible, and we left.

Good riddance.

And for the people in the back:

Appreciate Your People.

If you have a great teacher, great parents, great friends- great police officers- ANYONE- appreciate them.

Love them and if something is wrong- TELL THEM.

They will go to bat for you.

My mom would have taken out the entire district had I told her.

You do not have to suffer for years.

Talk it out.

If anything does not feel good to you- get a safe person- a safe space- and communicate!

Your people will be there. Your people will help you.

Be there for them too! They need you just as much as you need them. Be each other's PEOPLE. Light each other up!

We need to build together.

Normalize talking about weird stuff!

Cool things come from it!

Get curious. And always appreciate the people who make the hard times —even just a little less hard.

This book is dedicated to my wonderful elementary teachers who made learning fun and made me love school- love learning- and made me a student for life.

A special thank you to my favorite teacher- who gave me the hope- gave me light, through all of the darkness.

You are the epitome of what a teacher should be.

I am so blessed to have had you in my corner all of those years.

I can't imagine how I would have ever made it through without you.

Thank you for helping me keeping my spark alive through it all.

Thank you for being you and teaching me just how important that truly is.

There are no words that will ever be able to say just how much I appreciate you.

Thank you to all the incredible teachers and police officers out there.

Keep shining.

You are appreciated and needed more than you know.

This book comes with a unique, behind the scenes story.

I had a really tough time writing this story. I fought with a lot of it in my brain.

It's heavy.

Revisiting these stories- puts me right back in the moment.

I almost quit this process so many times, that I lost count.

I tore up the inside of my cheeks, biting them so much that Marco was worried I would have holes in them.

It was tough.

Was this really all worth it?

So I asked myself what I needed to get through this process.

What I needed was a sign.

I *really* needed a sign.

Even those of us who believe in ourselves 8 billion percent- still have tough moments. Moments where doubt tries to get us.

On this particular day- I was having a hard time leaning in.

My excitement was showing its face, as fear.

I needed life to show me I was moving in the right direction.

Marco and I have noticed that, when life wants to show you something, it makes sure that you are paying attention.

It is full of irony and it's comically bad. So much, that it's usually funny when you really think about it.

This story- is just that.

I had spent the morning with my mom, running errands. We were literally at, or next to, a grocery store all morning.

I never got the things that I needed for lunch.

I didn't even think about it.

When I look back at it- I was operating like I knew that I would be at the store by my house later that day.

It wasn't even on my mind.

My mom and I had a wonderful day and I soaked it in. Then she headed for home.

I went in to love on my puppies and check in with Marco to see when he would be coming home for his lunch break, and I had just enough time!

I jumped in Ronda La Honda and shifted my way to the store.

Windows down, music up.

One of my favorite places to be.

I pulled into the parking lot, and it was like I pulled up into an alternate universe.

Everything felt different.

It was like pulling up to a movie set, like the Truman Show (I love Jim Carrey).

I had to stop immediately.

The parking lot was pure chaos.

A girl had pulled out of her parking spot and driven up to the crosswalk. She was waiting on the people crossing when a handicap driver started backing out of their space.

The space that the girl was directly behind.

They were moving SO slowly.

Rolling closer and closer to the girl's car.

The girl couldn't move anywhere.

There were people everywhere.

All of the people stop- seeing it happen- but nobody moves.

Everyone is now frozen in fear watching this white SUV slow roll towards the girl's car.

The girl's mouth is open wide in shock at what is happening.

There is a heavy-set man outside the front doors with his hands on his cheeks- mouth open- face turning red because he has stopped breathing while watching this happen.

And then, JUST before the SUV collides with the girl's car at approximately .003 miles per hour, the SUV comes to a very dramatic halt.

I laughed.

I wasn't expecting so much flair!

Then it got better.

It felt like a circus.

The man realizes that he hasn't been breathing and starts taking hyperventilating breaths. He steals the scene with a gigantic hand sweep across his forehead.

"Whew! "

He mouths to the girl.

She relaxes now too, appreciating that gesture from him. She nods her head rapidly in agreement. She even threw in a thumbs up- which, I appreciate on a soulful level.

I have so many photos of me as a kid – looking like I am constantly hitchhiking because I always snuck in a thumbs up.

I was having such a moment with that thumbs up-
that it caught me off guard when all of a sudden it
felt like someone yelled out, "Annndd- Scene!"

Everyone started walking and moving like the
cameras were off them.

Back to normal.

And then I looked straight ahead.

And there she was.

My fourth-grade teacher.

Standing by her cart, in front of my car, with her
hands up in front of her chest- palms facing me.

And she mouths two words to me.

Clear as day.

There is no mistaking what she said.

"I'm. Sorry."

I sat there.

Mouth open.

Shocked.

And poof.

She was gone.

I realized; she took this batch of trauma with her.

I felt lighter.

I felt free.

I felt more myself than I ever have.

This story- this is the one.

This story is what changes my entire life.

It changed it before, and it changes it again.

But this time, it's beautiful.

I got my power back.

I let it go – right there in that parking lot.

Doubt and I would not meet here again.

Tom Petty came on.

Of course, he did.

I turned him up.

Windows down.

Sunroof open.

I shifted my way back to the love of my life and our next adventure.

"And, Scene."